Michigan Waves

Sarah Denton

Presentation by *BookLeaf Publishing*

Web: www.bookleafpub.com

E-mail: info@bookleafpub.com

ISBN: 9789358367164

First edition 2023

*Thank you to my amazing family and friends for
pushing me out of my comfort zone and
standing by my side through the thick and thin.*

ACKNOWLEDGEMENT

Thank you to BookLeaf for the writing challenge that pushed me out of my comfort zone.
Thank you to Emalee and Meghan for pushing me to do this challenge.
Thank you to my family for loving me always. Meghan, you are the best sister I ever have. Thank you for loving me through everything.
Thank you to my family, your love and support means everything.
Thank you to my amazing coworkers who let me write notes all the time to you!
And thank you to anyone who reads this collection, thank you.

Home

Mornings looking at the sunrise
Inching across the Mackinac Bridge
Cherry Festival, either love it or hate it
Hoping for spring, but having winter again
Itching for beach days
Going the distance for the ones you love
All the seasons in one day
Northern Michigan

Maple Tree

Strong roots spreading out deep underneath the ground, searching for water and nutrients for the strong maple tree.

Green leaves on branches that shoot up towards the sky, reaching out to the sun for nutrients and warmth.

Branches sway in the wind, dancing with the leaves, their partner swaying them around the dance floor as they listen to the music of life.

A strong trunk growing taller and taller, thicker and thicker, the tree won't be moved easily. The tree will stand tall and proud.

The old maple tree reminds me of days long
gone. Running around barefoot as a child,
saving worms after the rain, reading a book
under the shade of a maple tree.

They say it's just a maple tree, but I know it's
more. The bird nest with little eggs waiting to
hatch, this is home. Little bugs finding food
with the leaves, protection from birds in the
bark, this is a safe place. Under the leaves I sit
in the sun reading, forgetting the demands of
today, enjoying this moment.

The old maple tree standing tall and proud,
branches dancing in the wind, magic surrounds
the tree waiting for you.

Magic

She was magic and music, being near her filled your body with the need to move. She was love and joy, spreading kindness everywhere she went. She was fire and destruction, burning her path when crossed. She was a cozy day curled in the blankets, a quiet home. She was kayaking on the open lake, adventure seeping through her veins.

She sometimes forgot the magic she had inside her. Sometimes she was lost inside her own mind. She was a beautiful disaster, a masterpiece really. She was magic at it's finest.

Storm

The sky darkens, the air feels heavier. A rumbling boom off in the distance. Pitter patters of rain start to fall, light, refreshing, but only for a second or two. The clouds let loose, all you can see is the rain, the booms get closer, the storm surrounds you.

A warm blanket of sunflowers envelopes you on the couch, the low hum of the heater by you can be heard mixing with the rain pelting the apartment. The tea kettle whistles, it's ready to pour. A fun book keeps you company while the rain continues outside.

The torrents of rain comes to a stop, soon the light taps of a soft rain will stop. The sky lightens. A rainbow, make that a double rainbow fills the sky. .

A good storm soothes the soul. Washing away even for a moment the anxiety and self doubt, the feeling of failing at something, feeling alone and sometimes scared. Leaving in its path new beginnings, a promise for something better.

Memories I Don't Have

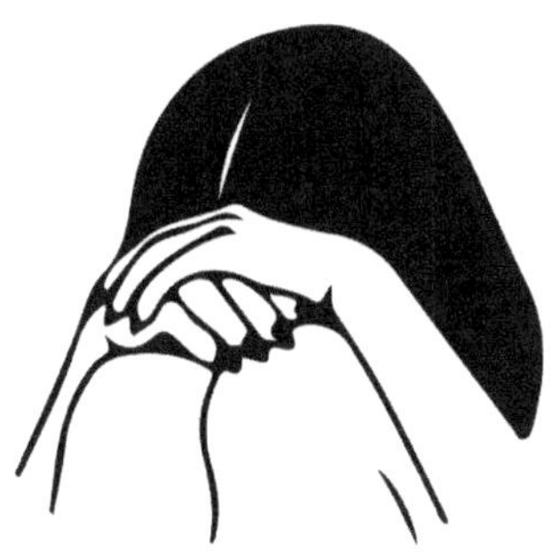

Hold me close one more time. Whisper my name and run your fingers along my arms as you memorize this moment. Feel my heart shatter as you tell me you're moving on, I'm not who you want. Let me push you away, look at my tears. Tell me you don't love me anymore, that maybe you never did. Give me the memory of you ending this. Let me call out to you as you walk out the door and I cry tears of pain alone in the room. Instead I have the memory of you leaving saying you'll be back tomorrow, watching you walk away and never look back because tomorrow will be here soon. You knew tomorrow you wouldn't be back, you knew my texts asking where you are would go unanswered. Now, I'm running into you around town, pretending I don't know you and you don't know me.

I wish I had the memory of us ending, knew why we ended. We don't always get the answers we want though. So this is me saying goodbye without ever saying goodbye.

Closure

I saw you yesterday.

I saw you yesterday at the store, I didn't know
you were back. Why would I? I didn't even
know when you had left. You're gray sweatshirt,
dark red beanie, laughing with your coworker,
brown eyes bright and dancing.

I saw you yesterday at the store, I didn't know it
was you until it was too late. I thought I heard
your laugh when I passed by, but you were gone,
so it couldn't be you. Standing in line you
suddenly appeared. You smiled your killer
smile, asked how I had been, my heart shattered
in the grocery store. Not strangers, but not
friends. You saw me cry yesterday in the
grocery store.

I saw you yesterday at the store, you've been
back a month now. Your line was the only one
open, I bought two gallons of milk from you.
You joked that I never had milk in my fridge, I
told you I needed it for soap. I called myself the
crazy ex to your coworker, then laughed as I left
this time instead of crying.

I saw you yesterday at the store, it's been almost
a year and a half since I first saw you again.
Almost a year since we ended things for good
after trying again for a week. Almost five
months since I last ran into you. You cut your
hair finally, your beard still long and full. A red
flannel, booming genuine laughter, I could see
your smile across the store. We made eye
contact as I walked to a register, a register you
weren't at. I walked away without looking back.
Did you feel the peace that I felt in my heart? I
wish you joy, I wish you peace and love and
laughter. I wish you well as I walk away silently
saying goodbye.

Wind and Flowers

Softly the wind blows
The flowers dancing along
Dance my love, just dance

Chance

Take the chance. Run. Fly as high as you can. Just take the chance.

You might crash and burn. You might wound your ego. But oh, how you might soar higher than you thought possible. You'll never know unless you grab it, run with it, take it as far as you can.

Take the chance. Just take the chance and see where you go.

First

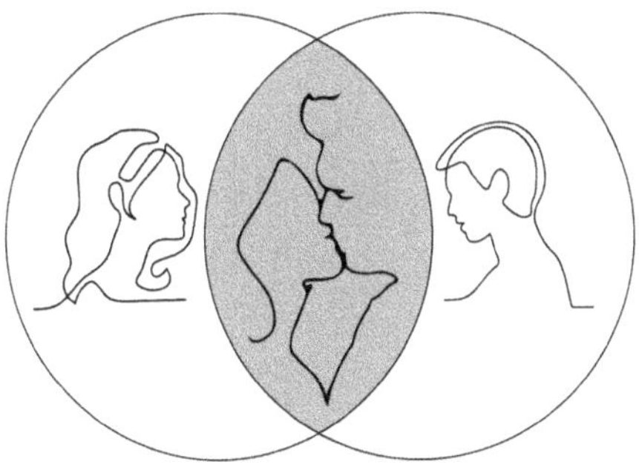

A first message, a let's meet for drinks, butterflies in my belly, finding twenty reasons not to go, and finding twenty reasons to go. The first hello, we're both so nervous, laughter awkward at first then flowing freely as the night goes on. A hug goodbye, can we do this again, a kiss goodnight. Turning on the car as he walks to his, why does this feel off? Why do you still feel his lips on yours? Turn off the car, yell out to him, kiss him one more time once you catch up. Tell him thank you, thank you for a perfect night while wishing silently for the night to never end. One more kiss goodnight. One more last first kiss, a promise this night is just the first night of many more.

Home

Big deep brown eyes looking at me, I can't help but stare back. In those eyes I can't help but see a lifetime. I see figuring out how to love together in a tiny apartment. I see buying our first home together, tackling random projects together. I see a beautiful baby girl falling asleep on your shoulder with the bright pink blanket on you both. I see watching cartoons on Saturday morning with our son. I see late night giggles together. I see arguments so stupid we have no idea why we started the argument in the first place. I see working together to overcome challenges, working as a team. I see laughter and new beginnings in your eyes.

I see home in your eyes.

Tiny Fingers and Toes

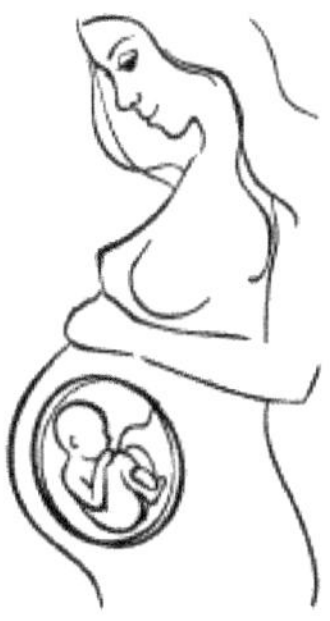

Tiny fingers and tiny toes,
Wiggles and giggles,
Big gummy smiles and bright eyes,
A baby so tiny, yet my heart is filled with love.

Ear piercing screams and the saddest cries,
Late nights pacing the hallway,
Silly songs and colorful board books,
This tiny human is my whole world.

The days are long, but the months speed by,
I never knew I could love someone so deeply.
No matter how big you grow, how far you travel,
you will always be my perfect baby, the love of
my life.

Little Girl

Little girl with her hair in pigtails running around the playground, dirt covering her face. Laughing, swinging high into the sky, wishing to never leave. Her mom calls out, "time to go"! She doesn't want to go, so she finds the longest way from the swings to her mom, wishing the whole time she could be all grown up, never having to stop the fun. Little girl, slow down, more fun will come after lunch.

Little girl holding her books tightly, hoping she will go unnoticed in the big new school. Kids rushing by, teachers in the hall watching for trouble, the bell rings a warning to hurry to class. She wishes for time to fast forward, ready already for middle school to be over. Little girl, the time is flying by already, just breathe and hold your head up high.

Little girl hiding in her room. Tears running
down her face, her heart breaking over and over
again when she thinks back to this afternoon
being dumped during lunch. She wonders if this
pain will ever stop. Little girl, breathe, he's just
the first boy of many, you'll meet so many who
are fun and interesting, changing your life in
ways you can't even imagine.

Little girl crossing the stage as they call your
name. Holding out your high school diploma,
the biggest smile on your face, dreams of college
and the future surrounding you. Little girl, be
proud of yourself, you did it.

Little girl, nervous about going out for drinks
with a new guy. Checking herself for the tenth
time before heading out to meet him at the
restaurant. He's nervous too. Laughing and
never ending conversation, the night never ends.
Little girl, this night is the start of something
magical and never ending.

Little girl looking down on her own new little girl. She's tired, but oh how alive she feels. Ten little toes and ten little fingers, breathing softly while sleeping. A kiss on the forehead, he looks at you with all the love in the world. Little girl, a family of her own, time is going to fly by faster than you know.

Little girl watching her daughter covered in dirt running and playing. She knows they need to leave the playground for lunch here soon, one more minute won't hurt. Little girl, call out to her it's time to go, watch her take the longest way to you. Time is flying by for you, but for her it's going so slow. Little girl, remember when this was you?

Little girl….

I Love You

Hugs that reach your soul
Kisses on the forehead
Send me a text when you're home
Send me your location
Squeezing hands
A favorite home cooked meal
A little note
A smile
Flowers on a random Tuesday
Being silly and weird together
Being called a dork
Feeling warm when they're around
Celebrating the good times together
Being there for the hard times together

I love you forever and always

Michigan Waves

Michigan waves pulling back and forth,
crashing over and over again into the shore.
The gentle swell pushing past my body,
laughter escaping as I forget reality.
My mind is calm, face up towards the sun,
laughter escaping my body as the waves come
and go moving around me.

Michigan waves pulling back and forth, crashing
over and over again into the shore.
Giant swells coming at me growing larger,
whitecaps forming, the waves knock me down.
Under the water I let my body flow with the
waves, coming up in a second for air.
The war inside my mind is raging between logic
and emotions like the waves growing and
crashing around me in Lake Michigan.

Michigan waves pulling back and forth, crashing
over and over again into the shore.
Sand and rocks beneath my toes, I sit back just
watching the waves roll up the beach shore
where they erase my footprints.

Giant waves or gentle waves, Michigan waves soothes the soul taking away the pain in our hearts and anxiety in our minds.

Michigan waves pulling back and forth, crashing over and over again into the shore.

Meghan Christine

When we were young my sister annoyed me.
Taking my toys, following me and my friends,
copying everything I said and did. Standing just
outside my bedroom doorway, but never in. At
night she would knock on the wall separating us,
her way of asking for a cuddle before sleep. My
annoying little sister.

As teens my sister stopped following me around,
she wanted to be known not as my little sister,
but as herself. Straight A student, honor roll,
never giving our parents a reason to be upset.
The exact opposite of me. But at night she
would sneak to my door, ask for a cuddle before
bed. My smart little sister.

Then came the early twenties. My annoying and perfect little sister was growing up. College. Boyfriends. Broken hearts. New jobs. New careers. Moving away. Coming home to visit, but never stay. My ambitious little sister.

My little sister is annoying. Smart. Ambitious. And funny, kind, honest, and my other half. She's logic when I'm emotion. She's a defender when I am weak. She's calm when I am a storm. She's my light when the darkness comes for me. She's my other half through and through. My little sister, my very best friend.

Coin

I am me. You are you. You say jump, I sit down. You say come here, I run away. You are you, and I am me. I say let's go for an adventure, you say let's stay home. I say let's see the ocean, you say let's see a movie. I am me, and you are you. Two sides of a coin, heads and tails. One is not complete without the other, we are a balancing act, our opposites complete us. You are you. I am me. Together we are complete.

Remember

If tomorrow doesn't come for me, remember:

Remember you are brave and strong
Remember you are kind and loving
Remember you are smart and brilliant
Remember you are beautiful inside and out
Remember your smile and how it lights up the
darkness
Remember your laughter is music to my soul
Remember that I love you more than words will
ever say
Remember that you are not alone, I'm in the
wind dancing alongside you
Remember that in the warm sunshine I'm
hugging you close

Remember that when the world gets scary,
lonely, or dark, I'm beside you always

If tomorrow doesn't come for me, remember that
I love you.

Mount Laundry

Mountains of laundry, dirty in one basket, clean in another basket. Dishes in the dishwasher waiting to be put away, dishes in the sink waiting to be washed. The bed is a sea of blankets and books, a fan humming along in the perfect corner. Half done projects decorating the table.

Tomorrow I say, tomorrow all will be done, tomorrow I'll clean my mess. Tomorrow comes and goes, the mountains growing higher. Tomorrow I say again, tomorrow is my favorite day.

Why do you let things pile so much? Why not take care of the mess before it's a mess? A million excuses comes to mind. I worked 60 hours this week. The sun was out, I needed to be outside. It was raining, the perfect day for a book and blanket. It was a hard day today, I'll do it tomorrow. All are true. And yet none are true.

I'm tired. Not go to bed early tired, but the deep in my soul tired. The tired that has you wanting

to take down the laundry, wash the dishes, you
know you'll feel better having them done, but
your mind is screaming no.

So I run the dishwasher and rest. One task a
day. Escape this life by finding a book to live in.
No matter how much my mind screams at me,
no matter how much I want to let go and forget
everything, I can't. I can't let the darkness inside
me win. I'm needed. I have a purpose. It might
take everything in me, but I will win each day,
even with the mountains of laundry and dishes,
the piles of books and half done projects. I will
win. I will live.

Look In Her Eyes

Look in her eyes. See the storm raging? See the hurt and anger she hides from the world?

Look in her eyes. See the burning hope? Hope that you won't let her down too like the others? Hope that this chance won't burn her like others have? Hope for tomorrow?

Look in her eyes. See the love and joy? See the gentleness and kindness? This love she has for every moment, every person, she gives so freely.

Look in her eyes. See every emotion, the pain and hurt, and the love and happiness burning inside her.

Look in her eyes. See the world, her hopes and dreams. Love her as she is.

4/12/2023

Backpacks, chairs, desks, books, games, a teacher's desk covered in paperwork and lesson plans. A whiteboard with today's date, a math lesson is forming. Teachers hiding students, quick texts sent saying I love you, send help. Fear and confusion fill the air.
Bang.

ATM, bank tellers, laughter, papers shuffling, keyboards clicking, money being counted. A meeting taking place for a loan on a new home. Today's date on the calendar for quick reference. Coworkers laughing, clients just needing quarters for laundry. A mother calling police for help, worried her son will cause harm at his work place.
Bang.

Family and friends gathering together to grieve the loss of a loved one stolen from this earth too soon. Laughter shared over fun and joyful memories. Tears flowing with the pain this person isn't here anymore. Love fills the air.
Bang.

Bang. Bang. Bang.

One hundred and two days have passed in the year 2023. One hundred and forty six mass shootings in the USA. Over two hundred people killed.

102 vs 146

I Wish You Well

Feel the sunshine on your face,
Feel the grass beneath your toes,
Feel the sun's warm embrace,
Feel the peace of rainbows.

Dance in the rain without a care,
Run through the meadow of flowers,
Listen to the birds sing with flair,
Lose time watching clouds for hours.

Listen and breath in the night air,
Today is over, tomorrow not here,
Hear the waves hit the shore,
Night wishes upon a star.

www.ingramcontent.com/pod-product-compliance
Lightning Source LLC
LaVergne TN
LVHW011309210726
843509LV00017B/2242